LIFE
SAVERS

ERYL
NASH

ANA
ALBERO

MAGIC CAT 🐱 PUBLISHING

NEW YORK

WHEN I WAS LITTLE, MY DREAM WAS TO BECOME A FIRST RESPONDER.

This felt extraordinary at the time . . . but today I am New York City Fire Department's first Black female deputy chief.

I love my job and feel privileged to be able to save lives and help people. It's hard work being the first on the scene of an emergency, and sometimes it can feel a little scary.

But the people I work alongside—firefighters, police officers, paramedics, and many other first responders—inspire me every day. Just like the incredible, real-life people featured in the pages that follow.

I hope you read this book and feel inspired to follow your dreams, too, no matter how little you are . . .

CHIEF TONYA BOYD

FIRST RESPONDER AND LIFESAVER

IN THIS BOOK, MEET
REAL-LIFE EMERGENCY
SERVICE HEROES
AND DISCOVER
EVERYTHING THEY
NEED TO SAVE A LIFE.

**FIREFIGHTER LEONIE
FROM THE U.K.**

Fighting fire on
the front line

**PARAMEDIC DAVID-LAWRENCE
FROM SWITZERLAND**

Traveling by land to provide
emergency medical care

**PEDIATRIC NURSE CECILIA
FROM SPAIN**

Treating sick babies
and children

**MOUNTAIN RESCUER FABIEN
FROM FRANCE**

Rescuing people from
danger in the mountains

**THERAPIST JOHANNE
FROM GERMANY**

Supporting adults and
children through hard times

**VETERINARIAN TAMIKA
FROM THE UNITED STATES**

Treating sick or
injured animals

**FLYING DOCTOR ANDREW
FROM AUSTRALIA**

Traveling by air to provide
emergency medical care

**SURGEON AHSAN
FROM PAKISTAN**

Performing life-saving
operations

**CANCER RESEARCH SCIENTIST
JIN FROM CHINA**

Detecting ways to treat
deadly diseases

**AID WORKER GABRIELLA
FROM ITALY**

Helping people affected
by disasters

**LIFEGUARD KOEN
FROM THE NETHERLANDS**

Patrolling beaches to assist
people struggling in the
water

A DAY IN THE LIFE OF A . . .
FIREFIGHTER

Hi, I'm Leonie, and I work for the U.K. Fire and Rescue Services. My day starts with a uniform parade, while the station officer tells me and the crew our roles for the day. In an emergency, one person might drive the fire truck, another might operate the fire pump, and others might enter a building to fight the fire.

Every day we make sure our equipment is working by testing hoses, ladders, and water supplies. It's important that our equipment is always ready so we're prepared for an emergency call.

As firefighters, we carry out life-saving work, but it's not all fast-paced. We work with our local community to teach fire safety, in order to increase awareness and prevent fires and accidents happening in the first place. We also take part in fitness training and practice procedures.

However, at some point, our mobile data terminal—a special computer in the fire engine—will light up. Within seconds, we're racing through the streets, blue lights flashing. We could be on our way to fight a fire, rescue someone from deep water, or contain a chemical spill. Either way, at the end of my shift, I go home knowing I have made a difference—whether it's making someone safer in their home or rescuing them from a fire.

LEONIE. DERBY. U.K.

When training in the drill yard, we pitch ladders against tall towers and use breathing equipment to practice entering smoke-filled buildings.

We practice using high-pressure hoses to put out roaring flames and use a hydraulic spreader-cutter to train for rescuing people trapped in cars.

When an emergency call comes in, we drop what we're doing and race to the scene to put all our training into action!

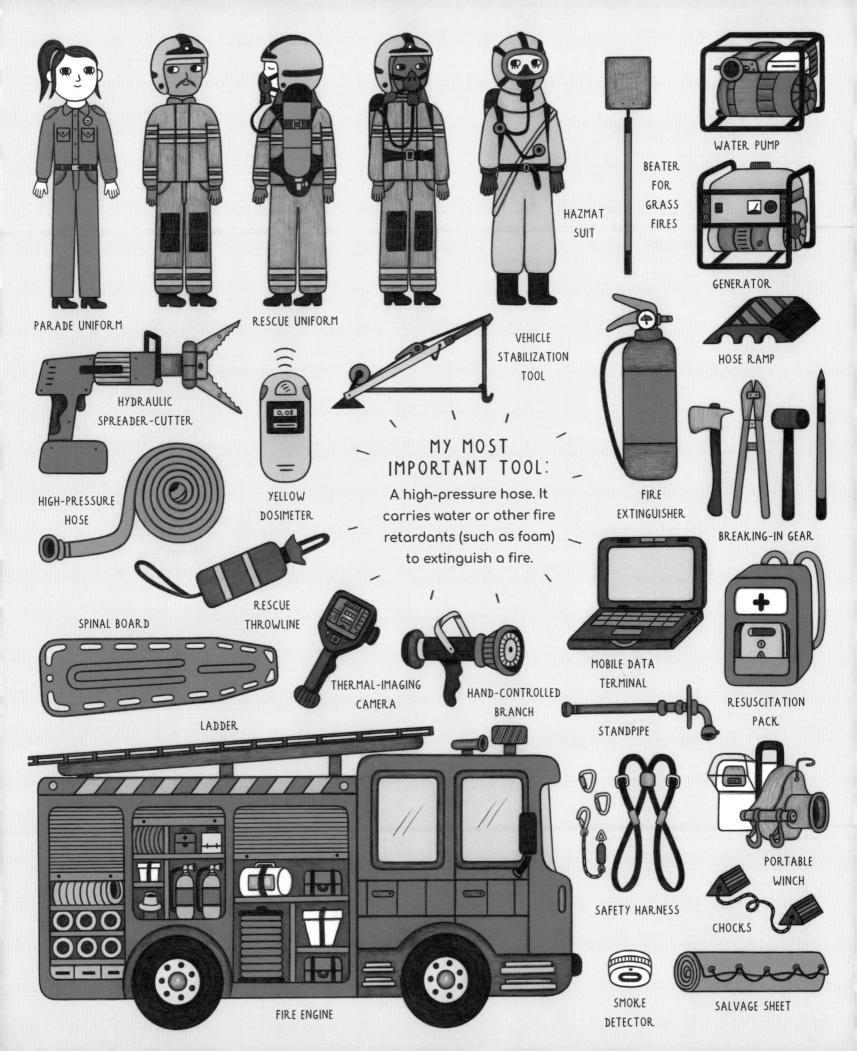

PARADE UNIFORM

RESCUE UNIFORM

HAZMAT SUIT

BEATER FOR GRASS FIRES

WATER PUMP

GENERATOR

HYDRAULIC SPREADER-CUTTER

VEHICLE STABILIZATION TOOL

HOSE RAMP

HIGH-PRESSURE HOSE

YELLOW DOSIMETER

MY MOST IMPORTANT TOOL:
A high-pressure hose. It carries water or other fire retardants (such as foam) to extinguish a fire.

FIRE EXTINGUISHER

BREAKING-IN GEAR

SPINAL BOARD

RESCUE THROWLINE

THERMAL-IMAGING CAMERA

HAND-CONTROLLED BRANCH

MOBILE DATA TERMINAL

RESUSCITATION PACK

LADDER

STANDPIPE

FIRE ENGINE

SAFETY HARNESS

PORTABLE WINCH

CHOCKS

SMOKE DETECTOR

SALVAGE SHEET

A DAY IN THE LIFE OF A . . .
PARAMEDIC

Hello, my name is David-Lawrence, and I drive an ambulance to provide emergency medical care in Switzerland. My day starts at the station as my partner and I check our vehicle to make sure the tires are in good condition, we have enough fuel, and that the blue lights and sirens work. Then, we're ready for action!

We receive information about emergency calls as text messages on two mobile phones. The messages tell us the address, the patient's age, and the reason they need our help. The call can be a category 1, 2, or 3, which tells us how quickly we need to get to the scene and whether or not to use blue lights and sirens.

As soon as we arrive on the scene, we let the control center know we're there. We make sure the area we're working in is safe and call the police if we need them—we're of little use to anybody if we are injured ourselves! If it's a public place, we also have to protect the scene from passersby.

The attending paramedic takes the lead at the scene, writing down the patient's history and current condition. The driving paramedic is just as busy, passing the medical kit to help stop bleeding or going back and forth to the ambulance to fetch equipment. We swap roles after every call and work well as a team. Our goal is to get a patient feeling better—and possibly save their life.

DAVID-LAWRENCE,
GENEVA, SWITZERLAND

When we get to the patient, we first assess the situation for dangers and quickly take the patient's history so that we can try and work out what has happened.

If a patient's life is in danger, we may perform CPR (cardiopulmonary resuscitation), which keeps their blood and oxygen circulating until we can get them to hospital.

With blue lights on and sirens blaring, one paramedic weaves in and out of traffic, while the other remains in the back to monitor the patient's condition.

At the hospital, we give a report to the doctors and nurses about the patient's condition so that they can give them the best possible onward care.

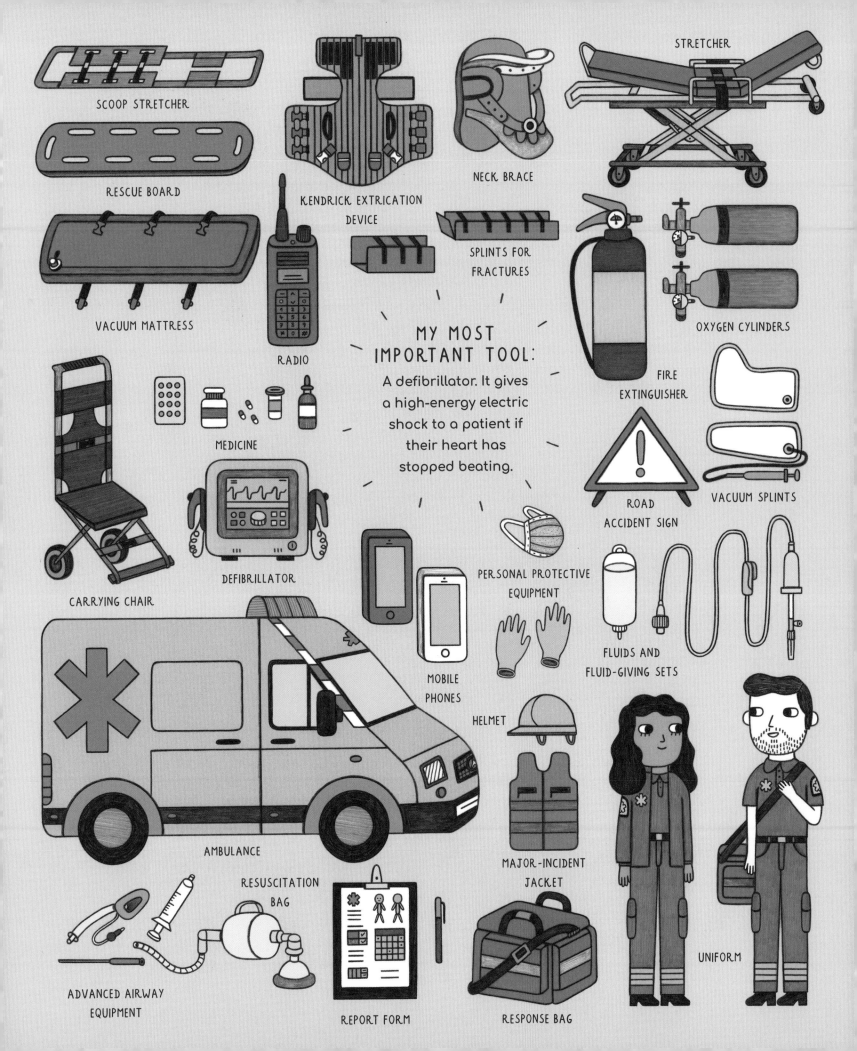

SCOOP STRETCHER

RESCUE BOARD

VACUUM MATTRESS

KENDRICK EXTRICATION DEVICE

NECK BRACE

STRETCHER

RADIO

SPLINTS FOR FRACTURES

FIRE EXTINGUISHER

OXYGEN CYLINDERS

MY MOST IMPORTANT TOOL:
A defibrillator. It gives a high-energy electric shock to a patient if their heart has stopped beating.

MEDICINE

CARRYING CHAIR

DEFIBRILLATOR

ROAD ACCIDENT SIGN

VACUUM SPLINTS

PERSONAL PROTECTIVE EQUIPMENT

FLUIDS AND FLUID-GIVING SETS

MOBILE PHONES

HELMET

AMBULANCE

MAJOR-INCIDENT JACKET

ADVANCED AIRWAY EQUIPMENT

RESUSCITATION BAG

REPORT FORM

RESPONSE BAG

UNIFORM

A DAY IN THE LIFE OF A...
PEDIATRIC NURSE

Hi, I'm Cecilia, and I work as a pediatric nurse in a hospital in Spain. Before I start my shift, I meet with the pediatric nurses who have been on duty before me to find out what the needs of each child in our care are.

I spend time looking after babies who have been born very small—so small that they can fit into the palm of my hand. We put them into an incubator, which keeps them at a proper temperature and helps them to grow and get better. Other babies may be born bigger but they can have problems breathing, so we help them by giving them oxygen until they can breathe on their own.

Some of the older children that come into hospital might have been involved in accidents and need to have surgery, or perhaps they feel unwell and cannot eat. We might give them medicine to make them feel better, or sometimes we carry out blood tests if we're not sure what's wrong. I work closely with doctors, helping them with anything that's needed, from changing bandages to getting them ready for surgery.

Parents get upset and worried when their child is sick, so a big part of being a pediatric nurse is finding the right words to reassure people and make them feel looked after. But our main goal is to make children better so they can go home and play with their friends.

CECILIA, MADRID, SPAIN

It's important that we keep detailed notes about the very small babies in our care to make sure they're eating and growing every day. It's a wonderful feeling to see them doing well!

I help children of all ages in various ways, from putting on plaster casts to helping fix a broken leg or applying a dressing to a wound.

I work across different parts of the hospital that are designed to treat children in lots of ways. I'm part of a big team of doctors and nurses who all work together.

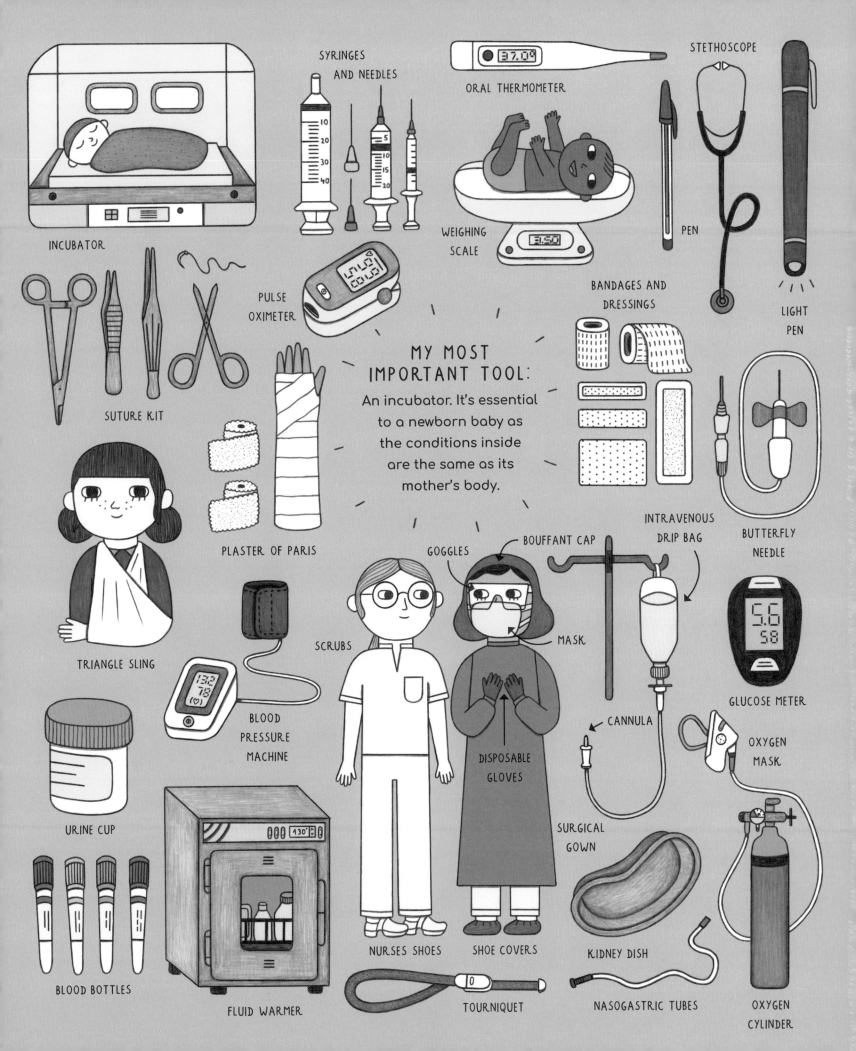

A DAY IN THE LIFE OF A...
MOUNTAIN RESCUER

Hello, my name is Fabien, and I work on a mountain rescue team based in France. In many countries, teams are made up of volunteers, but we are also gendarmes—trained police officers. We rescue people from dangerous situations, look into the causes of accidents and crimes, and help educate people to stay safe.

My week is split into time working at the drop zone, which is where our helicopters are based, and working at the office, where we answer emergency calls and organize the rescues.

A rescue mission can be by foot, by air, or both, with a team of mountain rescuers, a doctor, and helicopter crew. During a helicopter rescue, we carefully judge the terrain to work out how to get a rescuer safely down. Once we reach the casualty, we secure them with belays and ropes. The casualty might need first aid or to have their bones supported by a splint or stretcher. The helicopter then comes back to evacuate the casualty to safety or to the hospital for further treatment.

Many of the rescues are for climbing, paragliding, or skiing accidents. But no rescue is ever the same. We learn something new every time so we can be even better prepared for the next life-saving emergency.

FABIEN, CHAMONIX, FRANCE

Maneuvering a helicopter in mountain conditions is really challenging. Our crew has limits to how much weight we can carry and how long we can stay in the air, so we try to locate the casualty quickly and safely.

We use lightweight tripods that help hold the weight of a casualty to lift or lower them. A stretcher and a warm casualty bag then help us carry them off the mountain and out of danger.

We carry out around 1,000 mountain rescues a year, in an area of the Alps that has one of the highest rates of mountain rescue in the world.

There are 38 rescuers on our team—but not all are human! We have specially trained avalanche dogs that play an important part in finding people buried in avalanches. Their strong sense of smell enables them to find people covered in up to 6.5 feet of snow.

HELICOPTER

SNOW SHOVEL

RESUSCITATION BAG

FIRST AID KIT

EAR THERMOMETER

ICE AXE

WALKIE-TALKIE

ENERGY GEL

EARMUFFS

EMERGENCY BLANKET

MY MOST IMPORTANT TOOL:
An ice axe. I use the sharp point at the bottom of the handle to climb in very challenging terrain.

SPLINT

NECK BRACE

NAVIGATION SYSTEM

OXYGEN MASK

STRETCHER AND CASUALTY BAG

RESCUE TRIPOD

OXYGEN CYLINDER

SNOW ANCHOR

HARNESS

COMPASS

ROPES

CARABINERS

MOUNTAINEERING EQUIPMENT

HELMET

GOGGLES

GLOVES

RESCUE WORKER

PILOT

WINCH OPERATOR

SNOW BOOTS

SKIS

AVALANCHE DOG

ANIMAL CARRIER

THERAPIST

Hi, I'm Johanne, a therapist working in a clinic in Germany. I support adults and children who are struggling with difficult feelings by giving them time and space to talk to someone who will listen. I try to make them feel better and perhaps see the world a little bit differently.

The first thing I do when I get to work is check my answering machine and emails. My day is usually made up of five therapy sessions, and in between appointments I make phone calls and fill out paperwork to keep track of my patients' progress. Therapy is a two-way process, and it's up to my patients if they want to engage—some people might talk for the whole hour and others might sit in silence. It can take a while for someone to open up.

Communication is a powerful tool in my role, but I also use other ways of helping someone process an experience or emotion. If a child has experienced the death of someone close to them, I help them put together a memory box with items that remind them of their special person. If they feel worried, I help them write down their fears and feed them to a worry eater, a toy monster that can gobble up all their troubles!

One of the greatest rewards of my job is seeing someone at the end of their therapy journey who is in a happier place than when we first met. It's an emotionally demanding job, but every day is different as I never know who I might meet next.

JOHANNE, BERLIN, GERMANY

I run adult coffee mornings for those who have experienced the death of someone close to them. Through therapy, I offer support to help them move forward in life.

In the afternoon, I run sessions for groups of children, which provide a safe space for children to talk about something they are worried about.

In the therapy room, I often see patients with anxiety—a feeling of worry. I will ask them to rate how they are feeling, using a number system. At first, they might rate their anxiety as 9 out of 10, but after six sessions of therapy this can drop to as low as 4 out of 10.

PEN

NOTEBOOK

ANSWERING MACHINE

BUSINESS CARDS

PLANTS

COMPUTER

COFFEE AND TEA

CHAIR

WHITE-NOISE MACHINE

MY MOST IMPORTANT TOOL: A table lamp. The lamp softens the therapy room and creates a calm, safe space.

MOBILE PHONE

BROCHURES FOR DIFFERENT ORGANIZATIONS

DESK

PATIENT RECORDS

TABLE LAMPS

PILLOWS

WORRY EATERS

FILES

FILING CABINET

COMFY CHAIR

APPOINTMENT DIARY

TISSUES

MEMORY BOX

20   24

A DAY IN THE LIFE OF A . . .
VETERINARIAN

Hello, my name is Tamika, and I diagnose and treat sick or injured animals in the United States. When I arrive at the practice in the morning, I gather with my team to look at what we have planned for the day ahead.

Most animals come in for routine appointments, such as vaccinations, blood tests, or treating things like itchy skin or ear infections, but if an animal is very sick it might have to be kept in for longer. If that's the case, it is put on a drip, which is a line that connects the animal with medication and fluid through a needle in its skin. We watch these animals very closely and give them lots of affection.

Other animals need operations to make them better. Living in a busy city, I often see animals that have been hurt in road accidents. After looking at their X-rays and ultrasound scans to work out what is wrong, we put them to sleep using a special gas while we fix things in surgery. Before we start any surgery on an animal, the team and I get dressed in gowns and scrub our hands well to make sure everything is completely clean.

My working day can be long because I sometimes get called into work at night to see to animals that have become suddenly unwell, like an animal that has eaten a plastic toy and needs an operation to remove it. A veterinarian's job is never dull!

TAMIKA, NEW YORK CITY, USA

Since animals can't tell me where it hurts, my hands are really important for examining them, along with using specialized equipment to work out what might be wrong.

I've seen all sorts of injuries that require surgery, such as a dog with an appetite for eating socks and a guinea pig that broke its leg from jumping too high when it was excited.

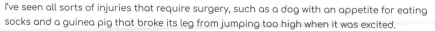

It's not very nice to see any animal in pain and how worried their owners are when they first arrive—but the best part is seeing how happy everyone is when they're reunited again!

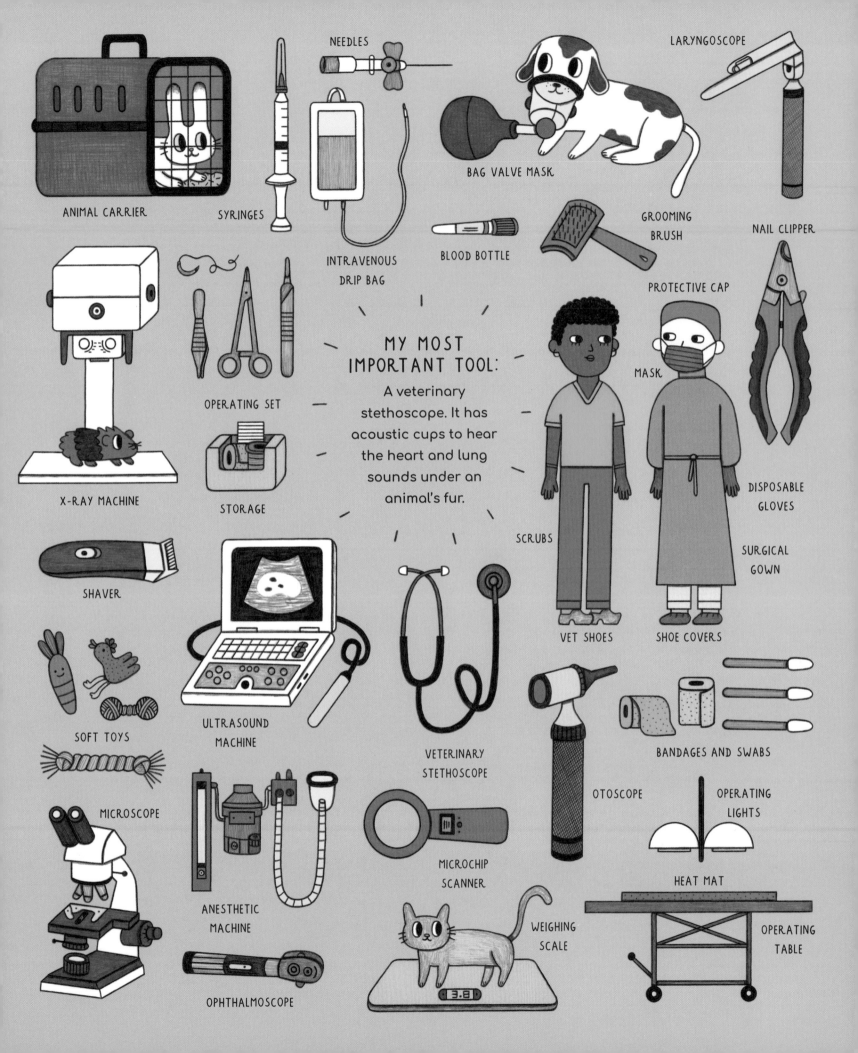

NEEDLES

LARYNGOSCOPE

ANIMAL CARRIER

SYRINGES

INTRAVENOUS
DRIP BAG

BAG VALVE MASK

BLOOD BOTTLE

GROOMING
BRUSH

NAIL CLIPPER

PROTECTIVE CAP

X-RAY MACHINE

OPERATING SET

STORAGE

MY MOST
IMPORTANT TOOL:
A veterinary
stethoscope. It has
acoustic cups to hear
the heart and lung
sounds under an
animal's fur.

MASK

DISPOSABLE
GLOVES

SURGICAL
GOWN

SCRUBS

SHAVER

SOFT TOYS

ULTRASOUND
MACHINE

VETERINARY
STETHOSCOPE

VET SHOES

SHOE COVERS

BANDAGES AND SWABS

MICROSCOPE

ANESTHETIC
MACHINE

MICROCHIP
SCANNER

OTOSCOPE

OPERATING
LIGHTS

HEAT MAT

OPHTHALMOSCOPE

WEIGHING
SCALE

3.8

OPERATING
TABLE

A DAY IN THE LIFE OF A . . .
FLYING DOCTOR

Hi, I'm Andrew, a flying doctor based in the Northern Territory of Australia. The crew and I fly from our base to help people who can't travel any other way to get the medical care they urgently need.

We tend to all sorts of patients, but most of the calls are for intensive care transport, when we fly to a remote place and transfer a patient to a hospital. If someone needs our help it means they are very sick and may need a ventilator to help them breathe.

When we've secured them at the back of the plane, we take off again to the nearest airport. From there, we continue the journey by road to the hospital.

We also receive primary trauma calls, which is when we're needed at the scene of a remote incident, such as a road accident. For this, we usually fly in a helicopter instead of a plane. This means we can land nearer to the scene and also on a hospital's roof.

No matter what the call is for, as soon as we get back to base we go through the paperwork and discuss what went well and what could have gone better. Then we check our equipment is well stocked so that we're ready for the next person that needs us.

ANDREW, ALICE SPRINGS, AUSTRALIA

We keep in contact with our base by satellite phone. It means we can be updated on how the patient is doing and that our base knows where we are while we're in the air. We often land in such remote parts of Australia that there isn't even a runway!

When we reach the patient, they are immediately moved onto the plane. If we're concerned about their neck or spine, we place them on a spinal board, using a neck brace and leg braces to keep them stable for the journey.

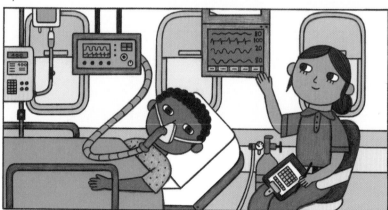

Some patients need medical care during the journey to the hospital so the plane is stocked with life-saving equipment, such as ventilators to help people breathe when they can't breathe on their own.

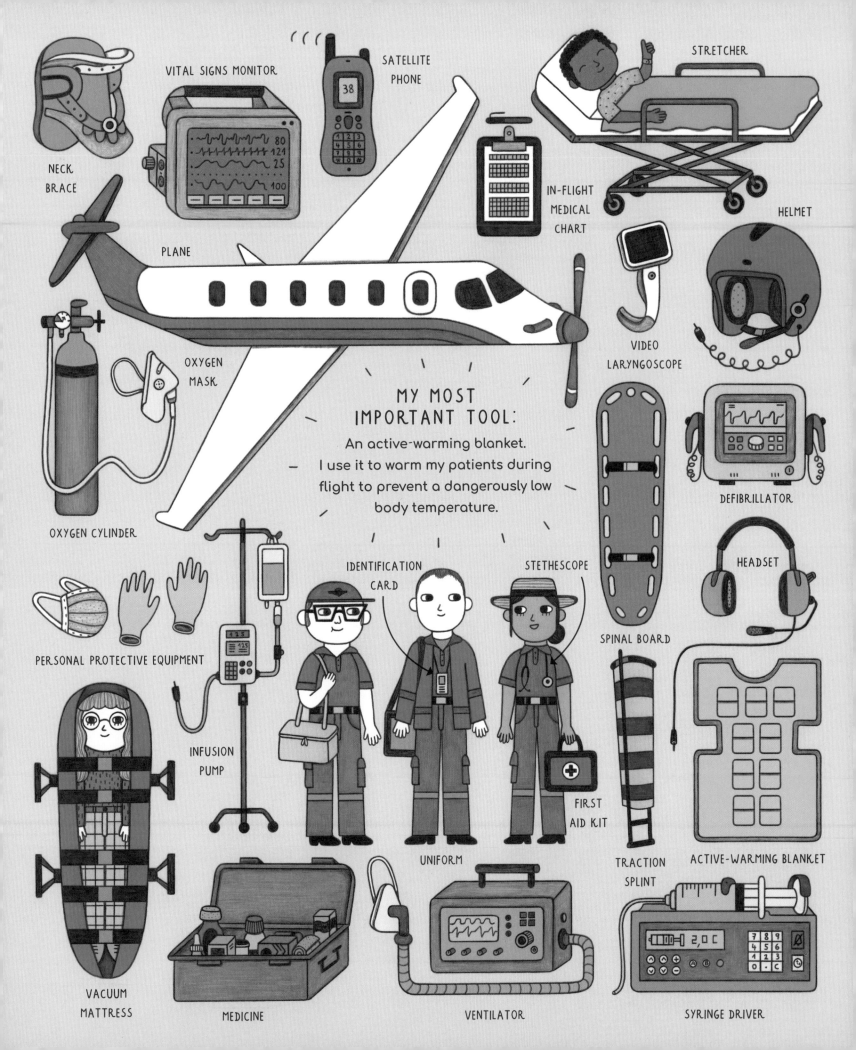

NECK BRACE

VITAL SIGNS MONITOR

SATELLITE PHONE

STRETCHER

IN-FLIGHT MEDICAL CHART

HELMET

PLANE

VIDEO LARYNGOSCOPE

OXYGEN MASK

MY MOST IMPORTANT TOOL:
An active-warming blanket.
I use it to warm my patients during flight to prevent a dangerously low body temperature.

DEFIBRILLATOR

OXYGEN CYLINDER

PERSONAL PROTECTIVE EQUIPMENT

IDENTIFICATION CARD

STETHESCOPE

HEADSET

SPINAL BOARD

INFUSION PUMP

FIRST AID KIT

ACTIVE-WARMING BLANKET

VACUUM MATTRESS

UNIFORM

TRACTION SPLINT

MEDICINE

VENTILATOR

SYRINGE DRIVER

A DAY IN THE LIFE OF A . . .
SURGEON

Hello, my name is Ahsan, and I'm a surgeon working in a hospital in Pakistan. I perform operations on people who aren't feeling well. When I arrive at work in the morning, I visit patients who have been staying overnight to see how they're feeling after their operation, which is called making rounds.

I have days when I carry out operations and other days when I take part in medical research, fill in paperwork, plan for operations, or meet new patients. Before an operation is booked, we carry out tests and use equipment like X-ray machines to make sure the patient gets the right treatment. If their problem does need an operation, I tell them what will happen during surgery and answer any questions.

I can perform between one and three operations a day, and they can last anywhere from a few minutes to many hours. A patient is usually put to sleep before they enter the operating room, using something called an anesthetic, and during the operation they receive air from a breathing mask.

Once inside the operating room, I rely on technicians and nurses to pass me the tools I need. They also monitor how the patient is doing as I operate. It's a team effort to make sure everything runs smoothly and help a patient feel better.

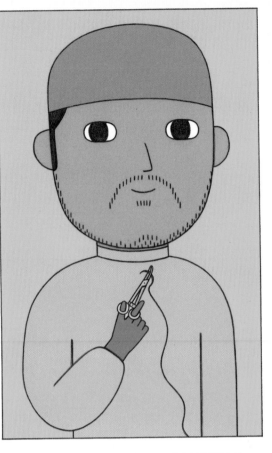

AHSAN, ISLAMABAD, PAKISTAN

Before surgery begins, an anesthesiologist puts my patient to sleep using a drug called anesthetic. The medicine prevents my patient feeling pain during surgery.

It's essential to clearly see the area that I'm operating on so we shine a bright surgical light onto my patient.

We wash our hands really well and dress in surgical gowns and gloves before we enter the operating room.

In the operating room, my patient's body is covered with a piece of cloth called a sterile drape, with only the area to be operated on uncovered.

Once the surgery is complete, my patient is moved to the recovery room to rest.

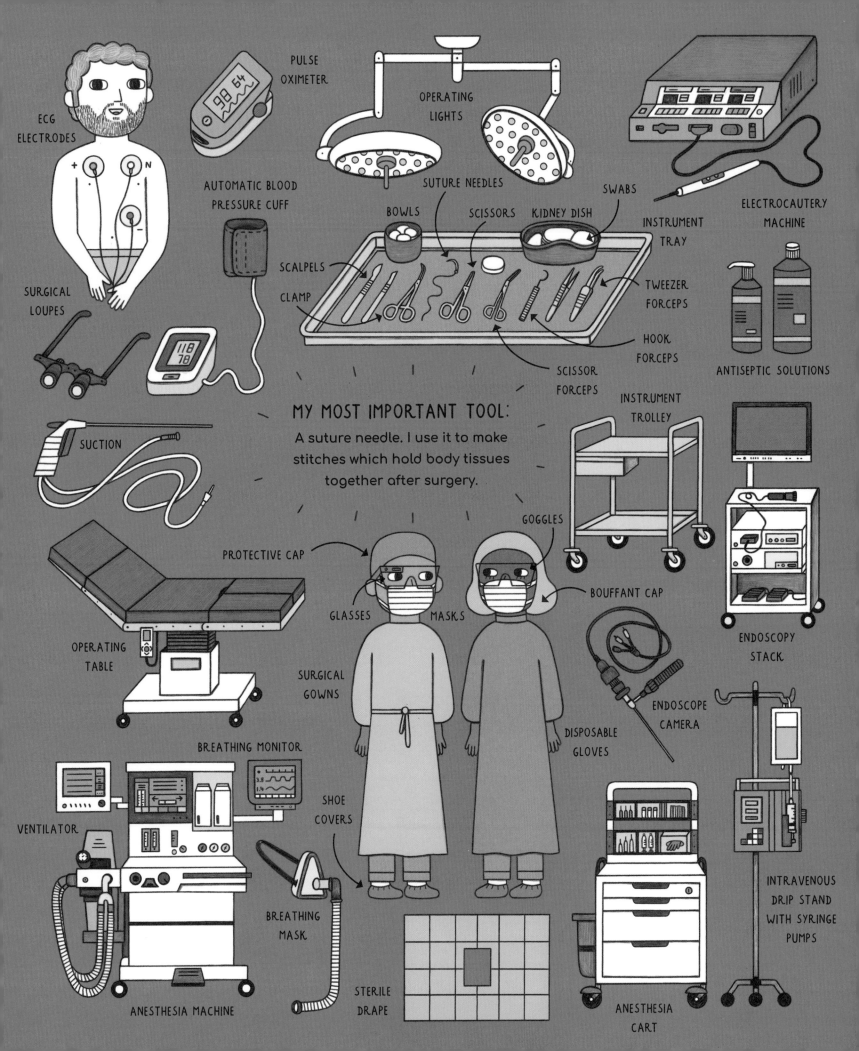

ECG ELECTRODES

PULSE OXIMETER

OPERATING LIGHTS

AUTOMATIC BLOOD PRESSURE CUFF

SUTURE NEEDLES

SWABS

ELECTROCAUTERY MACHINE

BOWLS

SCISSORS

KIDNEY DISH

INSTRUMENT TRAY

SCALPELS

CLAMP

TWEEZER FORCEPS

SURGICAL LOUPES

HOOK FORCEPS

ANTISEPTIC SOLUTIONS

SCISSOR FORCEPS

INSTRUMENT TROLLEY

MY MOST IMPORTANT TOOL:

A suture needle. I use it to make stitches which hold body tissues together after surgery.

SUCTION

GOGGLES

PROTECTIVE CAP

GLASSES

MASKS

BOUFFANT CAP

OPERATING TABLE

SURGICAL GOWNS

ENDOSCOPY STACK

ENDOSCOPE CAMERA

BREATHING MONITOR

DISPOSABLE GLOVES

SHOE COVERS

VENTILATOR

INTRAVENOUS DRIP STAND WITH SYRINGE PUMPS

BREATHING MASK

ANESTHESIA MACHINE

STERILE DRAPE

ANESTHESIA CART

A DAY IN THE LIFE OF A . . .
CANCER RESEARCH SCIENTIST

Hi, I'm Jin, and I work in a hospital in China as part of a scientific team carrying out experiments to help find ways to treat cancer. We look closely at cancer cells to figure out why some medicines don't work on the cells and what might work instead.

In the morning, a team meeting takes place where we talk about our projects. Then we get to work. A big part of my role is growing cancer cells using petri dishes or incubators. I look closely at these cells and watch how they change. I also run experiments to see what happens when different drugs are added or how the cells react to changing environments. It can be really difficult to find an experiment that works and then have to repeat the experiment in exactly the same way to get the same result. Working with living cells is unpredictable. It's a bit like when you drop a ball—you never know which direction it's going to bounce.

I do a lot of reading, too, because it's important to keep up-to-date with other scientists' work. We always think along the lines of "discover—investigate—share."

The best thing about my job is that the research we do could go on to save lives. If we discover something new, we might also end up with our work being published for everyone to see—which would be very exciting!

JIN, GUANGZHOU, CHINA

I look at samples under microscopes and see how they react to different drugs and environments.

Alongside the experiments, a lot of time is spent analyzing results and talking to the team about what we've found—and what we should try next.

At the end of the day, we store samples overnight in the fridge or freezer to keep them fresh.

FREEZER

COMPUTER

FORCEPS

MICROSCOPE

PETRI DISHES

CELL CULTURE
HOOD

MICROSCOPE SLIDES

INCUBATOR

SPATULA

WATER
BATH

SAFETY
GOGGLES

CELL CULTURE

MY MOST
IMPORTANT TOOL:

A microscope.
Microscopes allow me to
look at and study cells that
are too small to be seen
with the naked eye.

CONICAL FLASK

BEAKER

MASK

LAB
COAT

CULTURE FLASK

DISPOSABLE
GLOVES

AGITATOR

PIPETTE
FILLER

HOT BLOCK

BUNSEN
BURNER

TEST TUBE

EPPENDORF TUBE

TUBE RACKS

CENTRIFUGE

CHEMICAL REAGENTS

PASTEUR PIPETTE

GRADUATED PIPETTE

PH
METER

GILSON PIPETTE

WEIGHING BALANCE

FRIDGE

A DAY IN THE LIFE OF AN...
AID WORKER

Hello, my name is Gabriella, and I'm an aid worker traveling all over the world with a charitable organization. We provide money and assistance to people affected by disasters, such as earthquakes and war.

On a regular day my team and I meet in the morning before driving to an affected community. It could be a small village in a flood-hit area or a large neighborhood in a warzone, where the people living there are lacking basic necessities.

We make contact with the local authority or village elder on the way to seek their permission to help and let them know our intentions. It's essential that we learn and respect local customs as sometimes we arrive at an emergency with little knowledge of how people live day-to-day.

When we arrive, we talk to the community to find out what they have lost, what their needs are, and whether they would like our help. We can then work with them to put together a basket of important items, which tells us what things are needed.

We sadly can't reach every community. Even working seven days a week doesn't allow us to get to everybody. No matter the challenges, it's important that I remain patient in my job: A calming influence in a stressful situation can make a difference.

GABRIELLA, BUCCINO, ITALY

We drive to affected communities where people are often without many things we take for granted day-to-day, like food, clothing, and medicine.

Before providing money or goods, we have to check the legal process, seek funding for what is needed, and coordinate with other organizations.

Sometimes we provide people with cash, so that they can prioritize how to spend it, while other times we provide the goods themselves—it depends on the laws of the country, if markets work, and what people are comfortable with.

After a day in the community, we meet with the local authorities to share our findings and ask about any other needs the community might have.

A DAY IN THE LIFE OF A . . .
LIFEGUARD

Hi, I'm Koen, a lifeguard covering the beaches of northern Holland. My day starts at the fire station, as our vehicle has its own hangar there. I work in a pair, so my colleague and I drive to our post and discuss the day to come: What does the weather look like? Are there any special events we need to be aware of?

At the beach, we patrol along the sands, using our communication devices to keep in contact with other lifeguards on land and at sea. We give instructions to swimmers for where they can swim and keep watch over the water. Anything can happen at any second so we need to be ready for action.

Sometimes the pager we carry will light up to let us know there's an emergency. It could be a struggling swimmer who needs to be rescued or someone in trouble with a medical emergency on the beach. We're armed with first aid kits and rescue floats to be able to help as quickly as possible, and we keep in touch with ambulances and boats at sea in case we should need them.

After tending to the emergency, we start patrolling the beach again. As lifeguards, we're always on high alert: Making sure everybody gets home safe and happy at the end of the day is our main goal.

KOEN, JULIANADORP, NETHERLANDS

We patrol the beaches every day by foot, car, or boat. When our pager lights up, we know there's an emergency . . .

If someone's struggling in the sea, we throw on our life jackets and use our rescue buoy to bring them safely back to shore.

If someone has an emergency on land, we tend to them with our first aid kits. We use different types of stretchers to transport injured people to the our car or transfer them to an ambulance if they need to go to the hospital.

PATROL CAR

SURFBOARD

FLASHLIGHT

LIFE JACKET

FIRST AID KIT

RESCUE LINE

WHISTLE

RESCUE BUOY

MY MOST IMPORTANT TOOL:
A trauma bear. It has a calming effect on those in need of a big hug.

UNIFORM

BINOCULARS

RESCUE TUBE

STRETCHER

TRAUMA BEAR

WALKIE-TALKIES

22   22

EMERGENCY AT THE PIER

PAGER

AUTOMATED EXTERNAL DEFIBRILLATOR

DINGHY

COMMUNITY LIFE SAVERS

Community life savers are all around you—they may not be wearing red shorts or blowing a whistle, but they are making your world a better and safer place. There are many ways people help their community, from volunteering and freely offering their time to taking on paid positions, and here are just a few of these fantastic jobs:

ANIMAL FOSTER PARENTS

Foster parents provide temporary homes for animals who have experienced neglect, abuse, injury, or illness. They play a vital part in the rehabilitation of animals and help improve each animal's chance of finding a new, loving home.

BLOOD DRIVE ORGANIZERS

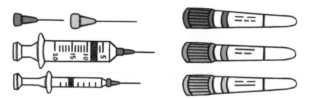

A blood drive is an event where people donate their blood for use in hospitals. Whether it is to maintain a general supply, or in response to a specific shortage, many people wouldn't be alive today if it wasn't for the generosity of donors.

COMMUNITY FIRST RESPONDERS

Community first responders deliver emergency treatment to people in their local area by attending emergency calls ahead of an ambulance. Having someone in the community who has been trained in first aid and can reach the patient quickly makes all the difference.

DISASTER ACTION TEAM VOLUNTEERS

Disaster action team volunteers provide comfort and care for families affected by major disasters such as fires, hurricanes, and tornadoes. From offering a shoulder to cry on to connecting people with housing services, they ensure that families don't have to face tough times alone.

FOOD BANK HELPERS

Food banks are a bit like supermarkets, but everything is free. Food bank helpers provide people with the food necessary to keep them healthy—they collect, sort, and pack food, and offer a friendly face to those in need.

HOME CARE WORKERS

Home care workers deliver care to people who require support in their homes. This could be due to disability, illness, or age, but caretakers meet various day-to-day needs, such as making meals, collecting medicine, or doing laundry.

MUTUAL-AID GROUP ORGANIZERS

Mutual-aid group organizers respond to the needs of communities. How they achieve this logistically differs from group to group, but usually people offer help—which could be resources, like food, or skills, like driving—that are then redistributed to those in need.

SOCIAL WORKERS

There are many types of social workers, and they help people cope with problems in their lives. The people social workers assist may be vulnerable, or in difficult situations, so social workers are great at understanding different points of view.

SOUP KITCHEN SERVERS

A soup kitchen is a place that provides free food, and they run on the kindness of people in the community. Volunteers make tasty, warm meals for hungry or lonely people, and most soup kitchens also provide other necessities, such as clothing and hygiene kits.

YOUTH WORKERS

Youth workers offer guidance and support for young people, helping them to reach their full potential. Their role could involve anything from planning a community event to bring people together, to helping those struggling with bullying.

Giving back to the community is something we can all do. It can help us learn about our own community, develop a respect and understanding for different people and lifestyles, and provide a fulfilment in having helped someone in need.

ACKNOWLEDGMENTS

With special thanks to the following real-life heroes
for their contributions to this book:

Firefighter Leonie Holt
Paramedic David-Lawrence Recher
Pediatric Nurse Cecilia Gomez
Mountain Rescuer Fabien Dugit
Counselor Johanne Schwensen
Veterinarian Dr. Tamika Lewis
Flying Doctor Dr. Andrew Ratcliffe
Surgeon Dr. Ahsan Naqvi
Cancer Research Scientist Professor Jin Lee
Aid Worker Gabriella D'Elia
Lifeguard Koen Hufkens

With additional thanks to the following experts who
helped with the research for this book:

Firefighter Martin Nash
Paramedic David Isaac
Pediatric Nurse Jennifer Campion
The Mountain Rescue Team at PGHM Chamonix Mont-Blanc
Counselor Sarah Bull
Veterinarian Dr. Alexa Montgomery
Cancer Research Scientist Dr. Josh Savage

RESOURCES

If you'd like to find out more about emergency service workers,
here are some sites for you to explore with an adult:

AMERICAN CANCER SOCIETY

The website of this 100-year-old institute is filled with history, research highlights, industry news, and everything you need to know about cancer research.
cancer.org

AMERICAN COLLEGE OF SURGEONS

Whether you're a patient yourself, dream of becoming a surgeon, or are simply curious, head to the ACS website for all the latest research, advice, and guidelines.
facs.org

AMERICAN COUNSELING ASSOCIATION

The ACA website breaks down what therapy is and how the therapists improve the health and well-being of our society.
counseling.org

AMERICAN VETERINARY MEDICAL ASSOCIATION

The nation's leading advocate for the veterinary profession, the AVMA's website shares a day in the life of a veterinarian, along with the training and opportunities available.
avma.org

THE BRITISH RED CROSS

If you'd like to be a paramedic one day, this interactive website is a great starting point to learn first aid skills with videos, case studies, and quizzes.
lifeliveit.redcross.org.uk

EVERY NURSE—PEDIATRIC NURSE

Detailing the skills and qualifications you would need to become a pediatric nurse, this is a trusted resource for nurses around the world.
everynurse.org/careers/pediatric-nurse

THE FLYING DOCTOR SERVICE OF AUSTRALIA

From detailed information about all the planes in their fleet to a live flight map, this interactive website is full of interesting facts about the work of these heroes of the sky.
flyingdoctor.org.au

MOUNTAIN RESCUE ASSOCIATION

Packed with information about staying safe in the mountains, you'll find everything you need to know about mountain rescue here—including what to do if you ever encounter your own emergency.
mra.org

OXFAM INTERNATIONAL

Here you'll find real-life case studies from Oxfam's aid workers' worldwide efforts to end injustice and poverty, as well as information about how you can help.
oxfam.org

U.S. FIRE ADMINISTRATION

With free materials to help increase awareness about fire safety, this website offers training to support firefighters in preparing, preventing, and responding to fires.
usfa.fema.gov

UNITED STATES LIFESAVING ASSOCIATION

Whether you're looking for advice about water safety or information about how to get started in a lifesaving career, this website has all the tips, stories, and guidance you could need to learn more.
usla.org

FURTHER READING

Busy People series by Lucy M. George
Emergency Rescue by Camilla Gersh
Emergency Vehicles by Rod Green
Emergency Vehicles by Simon Tyler
Heroes Who Help Us From Around the World by Liz Gogerly
Real Superheroes by Julia Seal

The illustrations were created in pencil and colored digitally.
Set in Ana Albero Font and Comfortaa.

Library of Congress Control Number 2021943157
ISBN 978-1-4197-4896-7

Text © 2021 Eryl Nash
Illustrations © 2021 Ana Albero
Book design by Nicola Price
Cover © Magic Cat 2021

First published in the United Kingdom in 2021 by Magic Cat Publishing Ltd. First published in North America in 2022 by Magic Cat Publishing, an imprint of ABRAMS. All rights reserved. No portion of this book may be reproduced, stored in a retrieval system, or transmitted in any form or by any means, mechanical, electronic, photocopying, recording, or otherwise, without written permission from the publisher.

Printed and bound in China
10 9 8 7 6 5 4 3 2 1

Abrams Books are available at special discounts when purchased in quantity for premiums and promotions as well as fundraising or educational use. Special editions can also be created to specification. For details, contact specialsales@abramsbooks.com or the address below.

ABRAMS The Art of Books
195 Broadway, New York, NY 10007
abramsbooks.com